GW00497856

A MANUAL FOR MANIFESTING YOUR DREAM LIFE

A MANUAL FOR MANIFESTING YOUR DREAM LIFE

HOW TO USE YOUR SUPERPOWER TO MANIFEST YOUR DESIRES

ERIC JOHN CAMPBELL

GROUNDED GROVE
PUBLISHING

Copyright © 2021 by Eric John Campbell

Published by Grounded Grove Publishing

All rights reserved. This book may not be reproduced in whole or in part, or transmitted in any form, or by any means electronic, mechanical, photocopying, recording, or other, without written permission from the publisher, except by a reviewer who may quote brief passages in a review.

Library of Congress Control Number: 2020921599

ISBN 9781087991023

CONTENTS

1

YOUR DIVINELY GUIDED MISSION

YOU'RE BORN TO BE A FREE AND POWERFUL CREATOR. It's your purpose here on earth. Whatever life you desire for yourself is wanted because you have the ability to make it a reality. All of your dreams are not far off fantasies that won't come true. Your dreams are instructions from the Universe as to what you're meant to manifest this lifetime.

You wouldn't have a desire or a dream unless it were within your power to make it real. You're the dreamer you've been looking for. There's no need to live through other people living a similar dream to yours vicariously. Instead of settling for an indirect experience, go for the real thing. You fulfilling your dream is the best possible thing you can do for all humanity and Mother Earth. Even if your dream seems selfish, trust that you don't see the bigger picture.

There's a divine intelligence that's beautifully harmonizing everything you experience in your world. A dream that may seem selfish for your happiness can have a positive ripple effect that changes the world. I mention this early on because I would like to remove any guilt you may have about pursuing your dream.

If you feel you need to take care of others less fortunate than you out of guilt, you bring more guilty energy into your world. On the other hand, if you pursue your dream with passion and joy, you're bringing those energies into your world. You must focus on your happiness and desires. If you try to find peace by taking actions from a place of guilt or fear, you'll find yourself experiencing more of these energies yourself.

Ask yourself: *what is it that makes me come alive?* Whatever that thing was or is now is the thing that deserves your full attention. It doesn't matter whether or not it seems practical. Keep doing it and think about it for no other reason than it feels good.

Whatever you focus your attention on will grow. Your focused attention is your superpower as a human being. The more focused your attention, the faster that thing will grow, so you must focus on what excites you. Your attention is what attracts the things you experience in your daily life. A great way to visualize this is to see the world as energy. Every single person, circumstance, and thing in your world is a type of energy that exists at a specific frequency.

Your life is like a radio station, where you get to choose what you want to listen to by changing your receiver's frequency. You're the receiver, and you change what frequencies you choose to welcome into your life based on where you focus your attention. By focusing your attention on a particular frequency, you become a magnet, immediately attracting to you all sorts of people, things, and life circumstances of the same frequency.

You're the creator of your reality, even if you attract things you've never thought of before. Your power lies in choosing which frequency you choose to set yourself at, and the Universe responds by giving you things that are an exact match to your frequency. It's essential to understand that attention means more than what you think about. Thoughts are part of where your attention goes, but it also goes towards the actions you take and your environment.

Attention is anything you focus on, which is why learning how to focus on what you want is the best way to develop your superpower of focused attention. You can choose to focus on things that exist on the frequency you're currently resting at, or you can focus on the frequency of your heart's desire. Your life's journey is shifting from the frequency you were born at into the frequency of your heart's desire.

Your journey plays out in all sorts of exciting ways in the world you manifest for yourself. Still, if you don't realize what's going on energetically, you may stay stuck at an unsatisfying frequency that attracts things to you that don't excite you and make you feel alive.

Everyone is born with a dream life that deeply excites them. The question for you isn't whether or not you were born with a dream. You were. The question now is: *do you know what that dream is, and are you focusing your attention on it?*

By consciously focusing your attention on what you want, you get to experience your power as a creator and not a victim. If you feel trapped by your life circumstances or past at this moment, realize it's because the power of your attention has manifested your current life to you. It'll be painful to acknowledge at first, but it's necessary to manifest your dream life. If you believe your current life results from things you can't control, you'll believe only circumstances outside of yourself can give you what you desire.

On the other hand, if you acknowledge that it was the power of your attention that created your current life, then you also have the power to manifest a new life by focusing your attention on something else.

You're the person and life circumstances you've been waiting for. There's nothing outside of you that's stopping you from living your dream life now. If you're ready to own your power as a Divine Creator, consciously choose to focus your attention on what excites you and what you genuinely want.

Don't try to get out of an unwanted frequency by thinking about things in that same frequency. For example, if you're in the frequency of being a victim, retelling your victim story repeatedly to find a way out won't change your life circumstances. Doing this will keep you at the same victim frequency, and the Universe responds by giving you things that match the frequency your attention is at.

It's also important not to deny unwanted things in your life. If you keep focusing your attention on your dream life, you'll attract everything needed to exist at that new frequency. If there are hurt parts of yourself that need healing, they'll show up in the light of your awareness so you may heal them. When these unpleasant emotions arise, you must meet them openly to get closer to living in the frequency of your heart's desire.

If you keep focusing your attention on what you want and then deny any unpleasant emotions that come up so you may heal them, then you're the one getting in your way. The Universe always gives you exactly what you need to live a life aligned with the frequency of what you focus your attention on. It's essential to become clear on your heart's desire, focus as much of your attention as possible on it, and courageously allow whatever comes up to enter your life.

As you begin this process, you'll likely attract things that seem negative and get you farther away from manifesting your dream life. If this happens, it's because there's something shadowy inside of you that needs to be brought to the light before you're able to live in the same frequency as your heart's desire.

You must realize that the Universe is never with-holding your dream life from you. It's never about earning favor with the Universe, so you may receive what you believe you deserve. The Universe wants nothing more than for you to live your dream on earth.

The only reason the Universe doesn't help you manifest your dream life now is, it's impossible to live a life you're not in vibrational alignment with. You must focus your attention on what you want so that your frequency matches your heart's desire; otherwise, the Universe can't do anything to help you get there.

The best that the Universe can do is continue to attract things, people, and circumstances to your life that match your current energetic vibration while creating a strong desire in you for something greater. You have to be the one to consciously choose to focus your attention on what you want to manifest. As you do this, the Universe will align circumstances in ways that may seem unusual to give you what you're calling in with your attention.

The Universe cannot call in something on your behalf because of the Free-Will you wholeheartedly agreed to before incarnating on this planet. You're the only one who can set the unseen forces in motion to attract the life you deeply desire. If you doubt you have this much power, look at how your attention currently flows and the life you're living now. You'll notice they're an exact match.

You have already used the power of your attention as a Divine Creator to manifest the life circumstances you're experiencing now, but not because you're a more powerful creator than anyone else and attracted people to you against their will. Every experience and person in your life was co-created alongside the Universe. It's impossible to have two people become attracted to each other as friends or lovers unless they co-exist at the same frequency.

You'll likely have to let go of some of the people in your life now as you become closer to the frequency of your heart's desire. As you consciously call in this higher frequency, you'll notice that the things, circumstances, and people you find yourself drawn towards will begin to change. Your favorite movie or book may no longer appeal to you. A friend you use to be close with may now seem like they don't have much in common with you. You may be scared at first because you'll have to let go of your old life before your new life comes in.

There needs to be a period of emptiness that creates room for new things to appear. You don't have to prepare for this transition consciously. The Universe will help this happen for you automatically by making you uninterested in things from an older frequency pattern and getting you excited about new ways of living, things, and people to be in a relationship with. Since this happens automatically when you focus your attention primarily on your heart's desire, I share this with you now so you won't get scared when this happens.

If you suddenly notice that everything you used to enjoy is no longer satisfying, you may think something is wrong. The truth is, this is the space the Universe needs to change your life and attract everything you desire. Without this change, your life would be exactly as it is now. To bring in a new life for yourself, you must first let go of your old life. There's no way around this.

If this process scares you, it's essential to focus your attention on your faith that the Universe is always carrying, nurturing, and holding you. The Universe may be invisible to the eyes, but that doesn't mean that the Universe isn't supporting you. You're a divine child of the Universe who's always being held. You have been held by the Universe ever since the moment of your creation here on earth.

Knowing that the Universe is always holding you will help you see that everything in your life happens for you, not to you. Everything you have experienced has been a response to the vibration you've chosen with your focused attention. Even the frequency you were born into was something that your Higher Self chose before you were born here on earth.

I share this with you now to remind you of how powerful you are. Everything you've experienced in your life is something you've attracted on some level. You came here on earth to learn, grow, and have fun. If you didn't learn how to manifest through your focused attention and instead were born directly into the frequency of your heart's desire, then your Higher Self wouldn't learn what it came here to learn.

Imagine a life where you get to have a dream, experience the contrast of not having that dream, and then achieve that dream through the journey of learning how to use your superpower of focused attention. You chose to be born here on earth, and manifesting your dream life is the highest potential you have for yourself during this lifetime. It's time for you to manifest your Higher Self's vision of heaven on earth.

Becoming clear on your heart's desire and pursuing it through focusing your attention on it is essential. Committing yourself to this journey will provide you with a feeling of deep satisfaction because it's the reason you chose to incarnate here on earth. To do anything else in your time here on earth will always leave you longing for something else.

You must pursue your heart's desire. By pursuing it with your focused attention, you'll learn what your Higher Self came here to learn, and you'll have the living experience of heaven on earth. There's nothing else nobler than following through on the reason why you came here. As you do this, you make the greatest positive impact possible for all humanity as you inspire others to follow their heart's desire and become living proof that it can be done.

Life can feel scary and paralyzing when you forget that your experience here is temporary. When you forget that your Soul lives on after death, it can feel like one wrong move makes you disappear forever. You don't have to carry this burden.

You're not alone in a temporary existence that can end with one fatal mistake. Instead, you live in a loving playground that exists to teach you how to use the power of your focused attention as a Divine Creator to manifest the life you dream of.

Fear is necessary because it teaches you how to go after what you want while trusting that you're fully supported. It's through facing and overcoming fear that you learn how powerful you are. You need something to rise above to see the power you have to rise.

Your Soul has a unique experience while on earth because you get to experience the manifestation of your dream life that directly contrasts the different life you were born into. You have a gift by being alive here on earth. Your Soul chose this gift enthusiastically, knowing that you would forget all this so you could remember again.

2

FEAR IS YOUR TEACHER

FEAR IS A FORCE THAT'S GREAT TO UNDERSTAND. Realize that fear is here to help you. There's no need to run away from your fear. Fear is a gift here to teach you something. When you sense there's fear in your body, become curious about it. *How do you know that you're feeling fear? Where in your body is this fear? Does the fear last for a long time or go away quickly?*

Fear can seem like this giant monster that's always chasing after you if you keep running from it. On the other hand, if you turn around and look at your fear in the eyes, you'll notice it can't harm you. Fear itself is harmless. The only time people get harmed from fear is while they're running from it. If you try to run away from your fear, you might do something regretful. Even that is only creating a seemingly harmful experience that exists to teach you something.

Whether you run from your fear or face your fear, you're learning. You're always learning while alive here on earth. You may be on a spiritual, business, or athletic path. Whatever path you're on doesn't matter. You're always learning, which is an important reason why you chose to incarnate on earth.

I bring up your relationship with fear now because your earthly experience will be far more enjoyable if you don't use it running from fear. Fear is an illusion that you can expose through curiosity and stillness. *Why is fear so scary to you?* The answer to this question can only be felt in the body and not answered with the mind.

This chapter may feel a bit heavy to you now, but that's only because of the part of yourself that believes fear is real. It's time to learn the truth about fear and how fear is a pathway to love and joy.

You're a divine child of the Universe who chose to incarnate here on earth to learn, play, and live your heart's desire. You're an energetic being of pure light, having a temporary human experience.

To incarnate here on earth, you had to forget

who you are temporarily. You're not your name, your past, or your physical body. These things are your temporary home, but they're not your essence. Your essence is the Soul of pure light that lives within you.

Your Higher Self chose to incarnate on earth for the sole purpose of having the unique experience you're having now. When your physical body on earth is ready to die, then your Higher Self will leave your body and transition into the next phase of your journey.

When you go through this transitory experience, all the denser earthly energies, such as fear, guilt, shame, and anything of a lower vibrational frequency than unconditional love and joy, are left behind. You keep all your memories, but there are no heavier emotions and energies attached to them.

The fear you feel throughout your time existing here on earth is part of the earthly experience. This fear isn't a part of your Higher Self and doesn't stay with you when you transition out of this life.

Your Soul benefits greatly when you approach your fear with the mindset of curiosity instead of running from it. Fear is a motivating force that moves people into action. Reflect on your time here on earth and see how fear has been driving you.

Has fear been something that you've allowed to hold you back from chasing your dream? Or has fear from your current life motivated you to learn how to change your frequency so you may manifest your heart's desire?

Without fear, you would be much less likely to pursue your dream. Without fear, you would be more likely to settle for the life you were born into. If you never went after your dream, there would be no learning about how you can manifest what you want with the power of your focused attention. There would also be no experience of you having the contrast of being born into one life and then later experiencing your unique version of heaven on earth.

Fear is necessary to have the full experience on earth that your Higher Self enthusiastically chose. The most important question isn't how to make fear in your life disappear forever. The most important question is: *how are you choosing to respond to your fear? Is fear motivating you to pursue your dream, or is it causing you to stay stuck in your current frequency?*

Fear itself is a gift. Acknowledging this will give you great peace of mind and get you to stop fighting something that's here to guide you. The most important relationship you can have with fear is that it's your friend. You welcome the fear when it comes because it always brings with it a valuable gift.

If you have felt a lot of fear in your life, this idea may scare you because the last thing you want is to experience more fear. But what happens when you become friends with your fear instead of trying to run from it is that it appears significantly less often.

Whenever you feel any strong emotion, there's a message the Universe is trying to communicate to you. Emotions and physical sensations in your body are both a powerful way to move you to action and deliver messages. If you feel fear, the reason may be that there's a message for you to receive.

There's a widespread belief in your world that fear exists because it helped humans stay safe in the past, but now that you've evolved as a species, it's a burden that no longer serves a purpose. The truth is that fear is still present throughout all of humanity for an important reason.

Fear isn't something that serves no purpose. There's nothing in your life that serves no purpose. Everything in your life is there for a reason. You do not need to know all of these reasons since that would overwhelm your mind, but if something keeps re-entering your life experience, there's a significant reason why.

When something keeps entering your daily life through thoughts, people, or circumstances, it's because something wants to be brought to your awareness. If something wants your attention, it's because the Universe wants you to grow. If you're experiencing a lot of fear in a specific area of your life, that doesn't mean you should try to ignore the fear until it goes away.

Fear will only keep showing up if there's a part of your being that wants you to heal it with the light of your awareness. If something wants your conscious attention, it'll keep manifesting in different forms until you fully acknowledge it. The Universe is always trying to bring more love and joy into your life.

Remember that you chose to incarnate here on earth to learn how to manifest with your focused attention. If you ignore the fear that keeps entering your life, you'll miss out on a crucial lesson.

By now, you may be beginning to see why running from your fear is only going to create more of what you don't want. The fear will get stronger until you finally can't ignore it anymore. Your fear doesn't get stronger to torture you but instead to liberate you. If you acknowledge the fear and ask it what it's trying to share with you, it'll respond with a clear message.

Everything that happens in your life happens for you. Fear is no exception to this rule. When you feel this truth inside of your being, you'll realize that fear is a gift. I will repeat this many times because of its importance.

The way you look at fear directly affects the amount of joy and love you experience in your life. If you see fear as a pointless nuisance that continually interrupts your otherwise wonderful life, you'll never be deeply satisfied.

If you believe you must make more money, have the perfect relationship, or some other thing to make the fear go away before you find peace, then you'll experience constant discomfort. To find freedom from fear, you must integrate it as a part of yourself. You must see fear as a friend of yours and love that fear as it is.

It's essential for lasting peace in your life that you acknowledge fear when it arises instead of pushing it away. Pushing your fear away will make it come back stronger and more frequently until you finally learn the lesson it has for you.

The Universe wants you to be genuinely happy and wants nothing more for you than peace, joy, and

ERIC JOHN CAMPBELL

loving freedom, which is why it'll keep bringing fear into your life if you're not learning from it. To experience these high vibrational states, you must learn what you're here to learn. Everything you experience in your life is to help you grow. The sooner you realize this, the sooner you're liberated.

There's no need to deny the unwanted things in your life and pretend things are great when you feel unpleasant emotions. Everything you experience, regardless of whether it seems positive or negative, is to help you grow.

Everything you attract has a lesson for you in it. While you're here on earth, you're always learning. By framing everything as happening for you instead of to you, you're increasing the speed at which you learn how to manifest your dream life through the power of your focused attention.

The quicker you learn how to do this, the sooner you experience your Higher Self's unique version of heaven on earth. Switching the way you look at your life is key to taking your power back.

You can only be powerful enough to create your dream life when you acknowledge your power. If you believe yourself to be a victim to more powerful forces outside of yourself, that's precisely what you'll manifest.

You may believe this life is given to you because of your powerlessness when the truth is, if you're living as a victim, it's only because of how powerful you are that you remain stuck. You're the only force in your life powerful enough to stop yourself from living your dream life now.

3

GRATITUDE AND EXCITEMENT

YOUR LIFE IS ALREADY FILLED WITH SO MUCH LOVE and joy! If you feel differently, it's because you're focusing your attention on less enjoyable things. I know this because your entire world is created from love. The energy of love is the constant that runs through everything that exists in your world.

Love is right in front of you, regardless of what you're experiencing. For some, this love is easy to see, but it may be hard to see for others. No matter where you are in the world, love is present and all around you. Love exists in everything. Love is the substance that created your world, so having an attitude of gratitude is always possible regardless of the situation you live in now.

Given what we've talked about so far, it's easy to

see why being grateful for the things you enjoy in your life is essential. Because of your superpower, anything you focus your attention on grows, which means if you focus your attention on how beautiful something is, you attract more beautiful things.

You're not necessarily attracting more of the same thing you're appreciating, but instead, it means you're attracting more of that energy into your life. For example, if you express sincere gratitude for delicious ice cream, that doesn't mean you'll attract countless people offering you ice creams. It means you'll attract more things that please you since the energy of pleasure you receive from eating ice cream is what you're grateful for.

Gratitude ties together with what we were talking about earlier, with love being the only constant. If there's love in everything, there's always something for you to be grateful for.

When you express your gratitude towards the love surrounding you now, it doesn't mean you're saying you want more of your current life circumstances if what you genuinely want is a significant change to your life.

There's a balance between focusing your attention on your dream life and being genuinely grateful for everything present in your life now. It's a balancing act because going too far in either direction will cut you off from manifesting your heart's desire.

If you're only thinking about how great your dream life will be while also being disappointed with your current life, then you'll keep manifesting a life where you're unhappy in the present moment.

If you're not happy in the present moment, you'll manifest more of the same because most of your attention is focused on your unhappiness. To feel good consistently, you must primarily be focusing your attention on how great it feels to be living your life. You can't focus most of your attention on how great your future will be without reinforcing that pattern of always looking toward your future for happiness.

On the other hand, if you only focus on your present moment, you'll keep attracting the same. It's lovely to keep attracting more of the same if you live a life you love, but if that's not the case, you'll want to balance the joy of your present moment with excitement for what's to come.

Of those two extremes, focusing on being happy in the present moment is the most enjoyable choice. *But why settle for one when you're born to have both?* Life is designed to fully enjoy and be in love with this present moment experience you're having now while also being excited about what's coming next in your life.

The vital thing to see here is, manifesting your heart's desire isn't about obtaining certain things, circumstances, or people into your life. Those come as you're living in the frequency of your heart's desire. The experience of life you've always been yearning for is that single point stretching on for infinity where you're delighted in the present and excited for what's coming next.

Being grateful for your present moment doesn't have to be something that requires a lot of discipline. The more natural and effortlessly the gratitude comes, the more powerful it is.

Look for all the things you genuinely appreciate about your present moment, even if they seem small. If you feel tired and are resting on a comfortable couch, feel into how deeply comforting that sofa is.

You may have an overwhelming amount of unpleasant things on your mind or emotions in your body when you would most benefit from practicing gratitude. Instead of lying to yourself, and giving thanks for something that makes you upset, focus on something small that genuinely gives you gratitude.

If you're upset with someone for something they

did, you don't have to stop yourself from feeling upset by listing out to yourself why you love that person.

If you're upset with someone, allow yourself to be upset. And if you feel like it's time to add more gratitude to your life, focus on how delicious the food you're eating is or how great the water from a warm shower feels against your skin.

Gratitude has to be genuine to help you manifest the life you want. If you pretend to feel something you're not feeling, you may convince other people, but you can't fool the Universe. The Universe responds to your authentic energy and can't be manipulated.

Manipulating the Universe isn't something that most people try to do consciously. Still, subconsciously you may be trying to do this by saying you're grateful for things you're not genuinely thankful for.

The Universe loves you unconditionally and will never punish you for doing anything. If you become aware that you're doing this, there's no need to be hard on yourself. The Universe loves every single thing you do, which is why the Universe wants you to bring more mindfulness to what you're attracting with your energy.

If you find yourself in a low vibrational state that you don't wish to be in, find anything in your present life experience that you can be genuinely grateful for. You'll quickly notice that focusing your attention on gratitude for something, no matter how small, will immediately give you feelings of gratitude for other seemingly bigger things. Energy doesn't distinguish between big or small things.

When you're grateful for feeling the sunshine on your face, the energy you put out is just as powerful as the feeling of gratitude you would have if you had your first child. To you, this may seem like two completely incomparable events, but both hold the same potential for creating feelings of immense gratitude. The energy of gratitude has nothing to do with the thing outside of yourself that seems to be causing it.

Gratitude is an energetic power that you can tap into at any point. Doing so raises your vibration and assures that you'll continue to attract beautiful things into your life that make you feel good. Being grateful often, you become much more aligned with the frequency of your heart's desire and increase the rate at which you manifest everything you want.

If you begin feeling jealous of someone else for having something that you want, try refocusing your attention on something you can be genuinely grateful for at that moment. Doing this stops you from feeding the energy of being jealous of other people having what you want and transmutes that energy into helping build the life your heart desires. It also makes you feel significantly happier at that moment because the lighter vibrational states that are closer to the frequency of your heart's desire always feel better than heavier vibrational states.

4

LETTING GO AND FEELING

LIVING IN THE FREQUENCY OF YOUR HEART'S DESIRE IS an intuitive thing. If you allow yourself to do what feels best at any given moment, you're living in that frequency. Your body and intuition already know what to do. Manifesting your dream life isn't about daily discipline and sacrifice. If you believe that's so, it's because of a belief you picked up from people outside of yourself.

Stop looking outside of yourself for answers and instead go inward. Hopefully, this book serves as a mirror, and anything that you take away is you remembering something already living inside you. Don't take away any message from this book that doesn't feel true at your core.

Manifesting your dream life is easy. If you

believe that it requires hard work and putting in your dues, we'll shift that now. You create more of any energy you put out into the world. If you feel stressed, overwhelmed, and out of alignment while trying to manifest your dream life, you'll attract more of that same energy.

Remember that whatever you focus your attention on grows. If you have to work hard to get something, you'll have to work hard to keep it. Your dream life is the most effortless and natural state for you to be in. It's living in a particular frequency where everything flows to you naturally, and it seems as if a faucet of abundance has been left on for you at full blast.

You've seen other people live this way. It looks like for some people, life's effortless, and success comes from playing. You'll manifest your dream life in the same way. The more you play now, the more positive energy you bring into your life through your focused attention.

The critical takeaway here is that manifesting your dream life happens when you're in a complete state of being. There are no actions you need to take to attract your dream life. All you need to do is focus your attention on feeling and living in the frequency of your heart's desire now.

It's impossible to do nothing. You'll always end up doing something even if you have no filled out calendars or daily routines. As long as you're in the frequency of your heart's desire, you'll naturally do the actions that manifest what you want and turn your dream life into your new reality.

There's nothing wrong with being busy and having filled out calendars. Many people love doing that, and it's the best way for them to manifest their dream life, but the critical thing is where you're coming from.

The being must come before doing; otherwise, doing reinforces an unwanted state of being. It's the frequency you're in, in each present moment, that truly matters. A great way to look at this is to surrender the doing to the Universe.

Surrender everything that has to do with how you'll achieve your dream life and trust that your intuitive, natural impulses will know what to do in each moment.

Focusing on doing the right things isn't where you want your attention to go. Instead, focus all your attention on how your heart is feeling at any given moment. Tune into your heart often by stopping what you're doing when you feel heavier energies and breathe into them deeply. Try to feel what your heart's feeling. By focusing your attention on your heart in this way, you naturally begin to raise your being's frequency to match your heart's desire, which is the frequency you want to live at.

Living in this frequency doesn't mean your goal is always to feel joy and happiness. These are great states to be in that'll often occur when you live in the frequency of your heart's desire, but you'll also experience anger, fear, disgust, and sadness. All of these are human emotions that are part of the beauty of being alive. These emotions will come to you often as you live your dream life and tune yourself into the frequency of your heart's desire.

You may be afraid of these emotional states and hope to escape from them. If that's the case, this is a desire from your mind and not your heart. Your heart loves to feel emotions. To your heart, there's no such thing as a positive or negative emotion. Feeling all your feelings is what makes you realize you're alive.

Living your dream life isn't about eliminating emotions you don't like. Living your dream life is about being in a particular frequency where you allow yourself to feel and express everything that wants to be felt and expressed at any given moment.

When you do this, you experience true freedom and satisfaction beyond temporary emotional states.

Underneath any emotion, you're capable of feeling deep, undisturbed happiness. This underlying happiness is what comes to you naturally as your being rests at the frequency of your heart's desire. Living a life free from unpleasant emotions is a shallow life. It's impossible to live a satisfying life by only experiencing the emotional states of joy and happiness.

Your Soul chose to incarnate here on earth to experience the full range of human emotions. The deeper part of yourself wants to feel all the emotional states freely while experiencing an underlying sense of peace through them all.

By flowing along with your emotions, you'll feel inspired to take the right actions at the perfect time to make your dream life a reality. As long as you stay connected to the frequency of your heart, you can use these powerful emotions to make things happen.

Anger is a potent fuel to spur you into taking the necessary actions to remove yourself from an environment that's not helping you grow. Fear can be a beautiful catalyst for uncovering and eliminating beliefs no longer serving your highest good. Disgust can make you start to focus more of your attention on what you want instead of settling for what you have now. Sadness can motivate you to reach out and connect with others on a more intimate level.

All emotions serve a greater purpose in your life. Let go of the need to try to get rid of your feelings, and instead see that every emotion carries with it a beautiful gift. Emotions never have to be scary. Emotions only lead to unsettling feelings and move you to unwanted actions when you don't express them.

Expressing an emotion as soon as it arises will always feel satisfying to you on a deeper level, no matter what the emotion is. Only when you suppress your feelings can they turn into this scary, seemingly unknown force that causes you to do unfortunate things. The only reason emotions ever move people in this way is because they need to breathe.

Emotions need you to express them in some form to keep your body, mind, and Soul healthy. Not expressing an emotion is a form of denying an essential part of yourself that wants love. Every part of your being on all levels wants to be and feel loved. Your emotions are no exception to this. The more you allow your emotions to be seen and heard, the more comfortable you'll feel.

It's essential to have your emotions be seen by yourself and others. Doing this will allow you to feel safe and at home personally and in relationships with other people. You're a beautiful Soul. Every single emotion you experience is directly from the beauty of the Universe. All your feelings help make up who you are. If you repress and hide away a specific emotion, that's a part of yourself you're denying.

You can bring all aspects of yourself to the light now. It's time and safe to do so. Your emotions are ready to come out of hiding and to be seen by yourself and others. If you've been hiding some of your emotions for a long time, you may be scared of them. You may be scared of what you'll feel and possibly do after bringing an emotion that you've repressed for a while into the light.

It's important to remember how strong and loved you are. You wouldn't feel this call to bring an emotion of yours fully into the light unless you were ready and able to do so. The Universe loves you more than you can imagine. In the Universe's eyes, you're perfect exactly as you are now and will always be perfect no matter what you do in the future. Remembering this will help give you the courage to bring your emotions fully into the light.

It's safe to feel your feelings and share them with others. It doesn't matter how long you've hidden away or repressed those feelings. When you connect with your heart and make an honest intention to shine the light of awareness on these tucked away parts of yourself, you'll feel deep, profound support from the Universe in many different forms.

If you believe that you're ready to bring these hidden emotions into the light, you're ready. Bringing your hidden emotions into the light of awareness doesn't need to be a long, drawn-out healing process. Remember the power of your focused attention.

If you believe the Universe is powerful enough to heal these repressed parts of yourself, that's what you'll experience. Immediately after doing this, you'll feel so much freedom and relief, as if you've just let out a big breathe of air after holding it in for way too long.

The unique and specific way that you bring your repressed emotions into the light is something that you'll know intuitively. If you set the honest intention to do so, a path for you to walk will become apparent. But if you don't believe you can handle it, there's no force in the world powerful enough to convince you otherwise.

You're the force that's in charge of your life. You're the only one that can decide if you want to repress parts of yourself or bring them into the light of awareness. You don't need to know how to do this because the Universe will always take care of that.

Your role is to decide if you want to reveal and expose those intimate parts of yourself. Only you can make this happen. Nobody else can initiate or do this for you. Put your focused attention on the power you hold right now to heal yourself through setting the intention, and the Universe will guide you on a simple and clear path.

The Universe wishes you walk this path because the Universe knows it'll bring you feelings of peace, freedom, and joy like you've never experienced before. When you bring all your emotions into the light of awareness, you're ready to experience heaven on earth right now and for infinity.

5

THE ILLUSION OF TIME

Living your Soul's version of heaven on earth is only possible when you realize that this potential exists for you now in this present moment. Time is an illusion. Don't wait until you've attracted all the things you desire before allowing yourself to experience your unique version of heaven on earth.

The present moment is all that exists, which means your dream life is available to you right now. It's not about one day bringing what you want to you. It's seeing that what you want to feel from living your dream life is available to you now. You must tap into and feel this frequency first before you'll see the physical manifestations appear outside of yourself.

Don't worry about trying to have your mind understand this idea that time is an illusion. It can't understand this by design. Instead, surrender the need for your mind to understand and feel what these words mean inside your body. You're capable of choosing to live in the frequency that comes from living your dream life right now. You can change the channel of the energy you're choosing to receive at this moment.

With your focused attention, you can stop feeding the reality you no longer wish to live in and instead feed the reality that is your dream life. Your mind may be coming up with all sorts of thoughts about why this isn't possible. Focus on what your body and intuition are telling you. For this moment, experiment with what it feels like to hear words in your body instead of your mind.

Time is an illusion. You can choose to live in the frequency of your heart's desire right now. Attracting your dream life is about being instead of doing. You don't need to make more money, have the perfect relationship, or draw a large following before feeling what it's like to live your dream life.

Your dream life is a potential that exists for you now, at this moment. Like a radio can be changed to tune into a different station, you can also change the channel of what life you want to manifest. There are no powers outside of yourself stopping you from choosing the channel you want to live in.

Since you were born, and until the day you leave this world, you're the one that decides what life experience you want to have. Your life is a blank canvas that you get to fill with whatever manifestations you want.

As you tune into a specific frequency, you're then manifesting people, things, and experiences that resonate at that same level of being. What you choose to create at that frequency is something new that you get to birth into your world that has never existed before.

The design of your world is beautiful. Earlier, we mentioned that everything in your life happens for you, but this isn't true for everyone. It's true for you if that's the frequency you choose to experience. On the other hand, if you want to experience a life where everything is against you, then you can tune into that frequency and experience that truth. The important thing for you to realize is you always have this power over your life.

If you want to live a life where you're just trying to survive, that's what you'll experience, and you'll always attract circumstances where you're struggling to get by. If you choose to live a life enjoying endless love and abundance in every form, that's what you'll attract and experience.

You have complete power over your life experience, but you don't influence the experience of another person's life unless they choose to give you that power. You can have a beautiful and intimate connection with another while also having no ability to save someone who doesn't choose to save themselves.

You'll always attract people, things, circumstances, and experiences on the same frequency that your being is at. See this truth, and you're free to live your life as the powerful creator you're born to be.

You can choose to exist at any frequency you want at any given moment. All you must do is set a conscious intention to live in the desired frequency and then focus all your attention on what it feels like to exist at that frequency now. As you do this, you attract everything that's in resonance and alignment with that frequency. This visualization practice is how you manifest your dream life.

A critical thing to understand is manifesting the dreams you have in your mind isn't always what your heart wants. Before you can manifest a profoundly satisfying life, you must connect with the frequency of your heart. Many people have attracted the material things they thought they wanted only to end up disappointed and exhausted. What you seek is an inner feeling that has nothing to do with the outside things your mind wants.

Often your heart and mind are in alignment, but sometimes they're not. What's most important is that you're honoring the feeling your heart desires. This feeling comes from living in a particular frequency that you may choose to live in right now. You may not immediately surround yourself with the physical manifestations you desire by doing this. Still, on a deeper level, you'll be living in the state that attracts all the physical manifestations your heart wants.

It's an inside-out approach. The being must come first before the physical reflects what you're attracting with your focused attention. The most powerful way to get closer to living in the frequency of your heart's desire is to act as if you're experiencing your dream life now.

When you act as if, before you know it, you'll be living the exact life you were pretending you were a part of and attract seemingly magical circumstances that reflect your new state of being. There's a balance to be had here. If part of your dream life includes being financially abundant, you don't want to spend money you don't have now pretending you're more wealthy than you are.

In general, this is about acting as if on a feeling level instead of a physical level. *What does it feel like to be living your heart's desire? What does it feel like to have your dream life be here right now?* When you act as if you've already manifested your dream life, you're taking advantage of this truth that time is an illusion.

By acting as if on a feeling level, you're immediately becoming a powerfully charged magnet drawing to you all energies in various forms that reflect what you're feeling. What is typically the most challenging part about this practice is surrendering all ideas you have about how your dream life will manifest itself.

You have many ideas now about what is and isn't possible to experience in your life. These beliefs that you hold about how your world works create your experience of the world. If you believe attracting wealth requires time and hard work, you may be cutting yourself off from an opportunity that will allow you to receive a lot of wealth doing very little work.

Surrendering your beliefs and limitations about what is possible for you in this life of yours will dramatically increase the speed at which you attract the physical manifestations that reflect the frequency of your heart's desire. You don't need to make a big deal about creating the right beliefs. Instead, you'll want to go back to the experience of the world you had as a child.

A child is born with no pre-existing ideas about how the world works. When you revisit this way of seeing the world, you become an open door through which miracles may enter. The Universe wants nothing more than to give you the physical manifestation of everything that your heart desires. The Universe will always give you what you want if given a chance.

The Universe loves you unconditionally, which is why you must open yourself up to the abundance that the Universe is trying to provide you with at this very moment. The quickest way to do this is to live in the frequency of your heart's desire by acting as if you're living your dream life now while surrendering all ideas you hold about how your world works.

Immediately after doing this, you'll notice that some unusual things start to happen in your life. You may be scared at first because your world will become less predictable. This change is necessary for allowing new gifts from the Universe to enter your life.

You don't know the best way for the manifestations of your dream life to come to you. If you could write on a piece of paper how you want your dream life to manifest in physical form and then have the Universe follow your wishes precisely, it wouldn't be as fun and graceful as the Universe handling this part for you.

You don't know how the physical manifestations of your dream life will manifest. You don't want to know how. How is the job of the Universe. How isn't your job. Anytime you get caught up trying to figure out how your dream life will manifest itself in physical form, you limit the possibilities.

Have fun feeling your dream life and act on any strong inspiration that comes your way, but don't act as if you know how the Universe will manifest it. Remain open to all possibilities. You're a child of the Universe, and just like abundant and unconditionally loving parents, the Universe can see so much more than you can. There's an inherent joy that comes from surrendering the things you're not meant to control.

Your superpower of focused attention doesn't require you to control everything to manifest your dream life. Receive the loving support that the Universe so eagerly wants to give you. You're never alone, and you're always loved unconditionally! Allow yourself to receive this love by asking for it with the power of your Free-Will and focused attention.

6

YOU'RE ONE WITH THE UNIVERSE

YOU NEVER HAVE TO DO ANYTHING ALONE. THE Universe is always available to support, nurture, and guide you. You can never call upon this divine assistance too often. Every time you ask for support, you'll receive a reply in some form. The unique way that you communicate with the Universe is something that only you know.

You may get ideas about how to connect with the Universe from other people, but nobody else will ever understand your unique relationship with the divine. Your connection with the Universe is an intimate and nourishing relationship.

By connecting with the Universe in whichever way feels right to you, you'll always feel better for having done so. Your relationship with the Universe is a connection to a source of infinite love.

You never need to thirst for love, nurturing, or peace outside yourself because all those feelings can come through you as you connect with the Universe. The Universe has no limit to how frequently you can ask for support and how much you may receive. The Universe's abundance of every positive emotion is infinite.

You receiving these wonderful vibrational energies from the Universe doesn't take away from anyone else. You're deserving of this infinite love, and the only person that can restrict your flow to it is you if you decide you don't deserve that much love.

You can think of yourself as a child whose parents have access to all the world's resources. If you're determined to do everything on your own, the Universe won't interfere. But when you call upon the Universe for help in the unique and specific way you both communicate with each other, you'll instantly receive everything you ask for.

You may not receive the physical manifestations you ask for because the Universe can't manifest material things in this way. Still, energetically you always receive what you ask for. The Universe wants you to develop this intimate and meaningful relationship. It's through this connection that you'll feel true self-love.

Self-love is the most important gift you can give yourself. It's how you'll open yourself to receive all the gifts the Universe has for you. The Universe has infinite blessings to share with you, but you can only receive these blessings in proportion to how much you love yourself. If you limit the Universe's love by thinking that you're not worthy of it, you create your suffering needlessly.

The Universe not only has an infinite supply of blessings for you but also finds no greater joy than seeing you happily receive them in all their forms. These blessings often start with a feeling of deep inner love and peace that begins attracting all the physical manifestations that match the frequency of your heart's desire.

The Universe can't manifest the specific physical things you want if they're not in the same frequency that your being is at. Still, the Universe can help you change your frequency to begin attracting to you all the physical manifestations your heart desires.

There are no limits as to the number of blessings you may receive from the Universe. As you choose to love yourself more deeply, you'll receive more blessings in your life in countless different forms. Now that you know how blessed you are, it's essential to love yourself as fully as possible to receive what the Universe wants to give you.

Loving yourself is about seeing how beautiful every part of you is right now. As the observer inside your awareness, imagine that you're a mother, and all you're observing as thoughts and emotions are this mother's child. By doing this, you'll look at everything that makes you who you are with unconditional love, and the Universe will provide you with countless blessings because you're in a state where you can receive them.

You need to choose to love every part of yourself as unconditionally as possible. It doesn't matter if you've done a heroic deed or eaten a whole gallon of ice cream on your new diet's first day. As the observer to your being, you can choose to look at everything you experience through the lens of unconditional love.

Choosing to look at every part of yourself through the lens of unconditional love is a power that you hold and can manifest so long as you set the conscious intention to do so. As you do this, you'll have thoughts and emotions of self-doubt. You'll find yourself being too hard on yourself and others sometimes. You'll feel anger, fear, disgust, and sadness sometimes.

Loving yourself isn't getting rid of these thoughts and feelings. Loving yourself isn't denying your feelings and pretending they don't exist. Loving yourself is choosing to see everything that arises within you through the lens of unconditional love.

A nurturing mother won't tell their angry child that they're not mad or shouldn't be mad. A nurturing mother will witness their child's anger through the eyes of unconditional love. It's okay if you didn't experience this type of emotional validation and unconditional love as a child. You don't have to stay stuck in the belief that your ability to love yourself is blocked due to what you experienced in your childhood.

You can choose to give the love you've always wanted and craved to yourself. You have that power and ability right now. From the observer's perspective in your consciousness, choose to look at everything that arises within you through the lens of unconditional love.

The Universe has looked at you through this lens since the moment you were born and will continue looking at everything you do now and in the future through that same lens. But to feel that love from the

Universe, you must look at everything you do through the same lens. You can't feel the unconditional love from the Universe or any other source in your world until you see yourself through this lens.

You're swimming in unconditional love right now, but you can't receive it if you don't choose to love yourself. No source outside of yourself can give you the love you need to thrive if you're not open and available to receive it. As soon as you choose to love yourself unconditionally, you'll find an abundance of love everywhere you look.

Love isn't something that can only come from an intimate connection with a significant other or a healthy family. You can find love in the smile of a passing stranger. You can find love in the sensation of the sun touching your bare skin.

There's no shortage of love because love is everywhere. Saying you're not loved enough is like saying you're hungry while standing in the middle of a supermarket with plenty of money overflowing in your pocket. There's only an abundance of love.

There's no outside force to blame if you don't feel loved. If that's the case, blaming someone or circumstances outside of yourself will only keep you stuck at a frequency where it feels like love is hard to come by.

Love isn't hard to come by because love is present everywhere. To open yourself up to it, use the power of your focused attention to set an intention to look at everything that arises in regards to yourself, both inward and outward, with unconditional love.

If you find this hard to do, you can always ask the Universe for guidance. Although you may not fully receive the Universe's love, if you don't yet love yourself, the Universe can give you guidance on what you most need to know at this moment.

Your most important source of guidance on your journey is your direct connection with the Universe. The intimate and unique relationship you have with the Universe is something that no one else can ever understand. This relationship you have is your source of clarity in this lifetime.

Everything you have read here has come from the Universe and a place of love with the intention of helping you to remember what your Soul knows to be true, but there's no need to cling to the words in this book.

The answer to every question on your mind and heart can come through your direct connection with the Universe. Even if you haven't consciously been aware that you have a direct relationship with the Universe, you do.

Everyone has a direct relationship with the Universe in their unique form, and the connection you have is beautiful. Nurture this relationship through gratitude towards the Universe and a curiosity to learn how the Universe most wants to communicate with you.

You have a direct line to the source of all-knowing. The Universe isn't only aware of everything in existence and how it all fits together but also knows more about your own life and who you are than you do.

The truth is you're one with the Universe, and your Higher Self is one with the Universe. You're designed to call upon and ask divine guidance for help. You're not meant to do your life alone. You're meant to receive support on all levels, and the most important of those levels comes from your direct relationship with the Universe.

There's no need for you to go through an intermediary. Of course, you're welcome to and encouraged to do so if it helps you connect with the Universe. But when you do, it's essential to realize that the best teachers and intermediaries are only helping you connect more deeply and intimately with the Universe that you are already in a relationship with. Nobody has your answers for you except you.

Other people may be able to hold space for you to go within. Other people may be able to reflect something that your Soul is trying to communicate to you. Other people may remind you, just like the words in this book, to look within. But there's no single person, no matter how famous or wise, who has the answers you're looking for.

End your searching and find peace of mind and heart right now by remembering who you are. You're a child of the Universe and therefore are one with the Universe. Everything you desire is what the Universe wants for you. Call upon the Universe whenever you need guidance and choose to love yourself unconditionally, so you're open to receiving all of the Universe's infinite blessings!

7

YOUR LOVE CHANGES THIS WORLD

LIVING YOUR DREAM LIFE IS ABOUT MUCH MORE THAN your happiness. Your path is more significant than you. Everyone creates their world based on where they place their focused attention. But since most people are unaware of this superpower they hold, they default to manifesting the life that already surrounds them.

If you can feel the frequency of your heart's desire, you're a visionary. You see a different path and are utilizing your power to create this new path for yourself. Doing this will give you no greater joy. Satisfying peace comes from feeling that you're a child of the Universe born into this world to create your unique version of heaven on earth.

When others see you living your dream life,

they'll immediately begin to think about their dream and how they can start living it. You may notice that as you manifest more of the physical items that match the frequency of your heart's desire, many of the people currently in your life will start to get jealous. It may seem to you like it's a negative feeling you're bringing to others when the truth is you're liberating them.

The only person that has the power to manifest a particular dream life is the person who has that dream potential living inside of their heart. By activating that highest potential frequency in yourself, you remind other people of their potential.

As you change your frequency, you'll find that it no longer feels right to spend time with many of the people you spent time with in the past. They may say you've changed negatively, but this is something someone might say if you're becoming more aligned with your heart's frequency, and they're staying at the same frequency. If that's the case, it's essential to know that people come up with all sorts of reasons as to why they need to stay in their current frequency.

You can't change or save anyone else; it's impossible and will only cause turmoil that goes nowhere. If you're in a meaningful partnership, you can choose to change your frequency together, but this is a choice you both must make. One person cannot affect two people in this way.

The way you positively influence the world is by inspiring people with your life and creations. You can never choose which frequency others live in, but you can inspire them. You can be so genuinely happy and at peace that others begin to look at your life and wonder what you're doing differently.

Many people will be inspired by you living in the frequency of your heart's desire, even if you share no words with them. From this place, you're inspiring people on an energetic level. This world you're living in is all energy. The higher and more pleasurable your frequency is, the more others sense and enjoy your energy in whatever form it comes.

You're actively changing the world just by being truly happy and grateful. From this place, you become a beacon of light, like a lighthouse that reminds others of their ability to shine. Although you'll trigger jealousy in many people, this is a necessary catalyst for others to break free from being passive in their life and see that they can actively focus their attention on a different way of living, just like you.

You won't realize the full positive effect you have

on others while you're here on earth, so it's essential to hear from the Universe how valuable and necessary what you're choosing to do is. By inspiring one person to pursue living in the frequency of their heart's desire, they, in turn, may motivate a million more.

You're an incredible gift to this world. Pursuing your bliss on your journey is the best possible thing you can do for humanity. Anytime someone tries to convince you to do something from a place of guilt, remember that your ability to change the world and bring happiness to many more people comes from you being happy and deeply fulfilled first.

If you decide to donate or volunteer your time, do so because it brings you great pleasure. This world is all energy, which means the energy you're coming from and bringing into your world at the level of being is significantly more important than what you do.

You're a gift to this world just for being alive. You're a sun, and by tuning into the frequency of your dream life, you're removing all the false layers that have blocked yourself from shining.

Have you ever been near someone who was radiating? Have you ever been near someone who just made you happy, and you don't know why? The light that you witnessed in other people is the same one that lives within you. You have that potential inside of you now to radiate joy, not from doing anything, but by simply being.

Thank you sincerely for being here on earth at this time. You're an angel here to lift your planet's collective frequency just by shining your light. Shining your light is your purpose for being here on earth. You'll shine your light in a way that's specific and unique to you.

You must see the value in your light to confidently display it for everyone else to see. You radiate light just from being happy and loving yourself unconditionally. The fantastic thing about light is it dispels darkness wherever you go. Darkness is only scary because it represents everything that hasn't yet been brought to the light and seen for what it is.

As you reveal your emotions in the light of awareness, you purify all parts of yourself and remove the walls that prevent your light from shining. You're the only one who can choose to shine your light in this world. You may have picked up a belief along your journey that you don't have light to share, or your light isn't as powerful as the light in other people.

It's essential to realize that the light that lives

within you is the same light that lives within everybody else. You'll express this light in a way that only you can do, but the light itself comes from an infinite source that everyone is tapped into.

The feeling you receive from being this source of light for others is more incredible than you can imagine. You'll find that the people, circumstances, and experiences you attract are gentle and kind.

By being a beacon of light, you automatically bring out the best in others. You'll notice that the way people treat you is with great respect and joy. You'll automatically put others to ease in your presence because there's nothing for them to be defensive about.

As you shine your light fully, you're showering all parts of your being with unconditional love. This light you express is the light of unconditional love. As you love all aspects of yourself in this way, you'll find that you no longer judge others. Although people can never hear your thoughts, if you judge them, they sense it energetically.

As you shower yourself and others with your light, you no longer find satisfaction from judging others. Nothing threatens you when you feel this much love for yourself, and when nothing threatens you, you're not threatening to anyone else.

You may not want to spend time with people in a less favorable frequency as you, but when you interact with those people, you'll always bring out the best in them and inspire them to bring out the best in themselves.

Light attracts and brings more light. Everyone has access to the light switch of the light that lives within. As you shine your light, you remind people that they, too, can flip this switch on and share their unique version of the light with the world.

It'll be mind-boggling for others to see how people treat you. Many people who've built up a reputation for being mean or cold will be soft and warm in your presence. You'll notice that animals are more likely to come up to you and be comfortable near you.

As you become a bright source of light, you emanate unconditional love, which is why you feel so happy for seemingly no reason when in the presence of someone who's radiant.

You're born to be radiant in your unique way. You're born to bring out the best in yourself and others. When you connect with the light that lives within, you'll notice everything you experience on the outside reflects what you're experiencing on the inside.

Everything you're learning inside of this book is an inside-out approach. It all starts on the inside. When you feel peace and love for yourself, you radiate peace and love for all others, which is why pursuing your authentic happiness is the greatest gift you can give to the world.

You're not designed to fix others or care for them at the expense of yourself. It's impossible to care for others if you don't feel taken care of. Learning to love yourself first is how you express love towards the people in your life.

Don't try to love others if you feel unloved yourself. Giving love from this place will make you feel resentful because you'll feel as if you have a minimal supply of love, and because you're giving it up, you expect something big in return.

Giving love with the expectation of getting something in return isn't love. You can only share love unconditionally, and the only way to give out love this freely is to realize you have an infinite supply of it that lives inside. You never need to seek love outside of yourself, and ironically by being aware of this, you'll find yourself attracting love from many people.

As you give away love unconditionally, you'll also find that you receive love unconditionally from the many forms of love in your world. At the core, love is all there is! With this in mind, it's essential to make your priority loving yourself.

The most crucial step on this journey is realizing that you're the only one who can give yourself the love you need. If you seek this love outside of yourself first, you'll be let down often and become cold towards the world.

If you believe that there's not enough love to go around, it's only because of a misunderstanding you had when you were a child. When you see and feel the infinite amount of love that the Universe has for you, your perspective will shift forever.

It's impossible to believe love is limited when you feel it arise deep within in a way that starts to overflow onto everyone and everything that you focus your attention on. Seeing everything you do from this lens of unconditional love is the only way for you to love others. Loving yourself first is never selfish and always necessary.

Because of the power of your focused attention, you can start loving yourself right now. Stop feeding any old beliefs that say this is a hard thing to do, and use your focused attention to love everything that makes you who you are.

As you do this, you'll soon find that the amount

of love you have to share with others is limitless. This love you have for others can be given out freely without expecting to get something in return because you know you have an infinite supply of love available to you.

8

INTEGRATE WHAT YOU'VE LEARNED

As we begin the final chapter of this book, it's essential to discuss how to integrate everything we've talked about into your daily life. You may feel closer to the Universe now than ever before. The question becomes: *how do you keep and nurture this loving connection in your everyday life?*

The most important thing you have heard while reading this book is to use your superpower of focused attention by focusing on what you want to grow.

If you fall into a default mode, you might find yourself watching movies that instill fear or reading news articles written from a place of fear. Every activity you participate in requires you to focus your attention on one specific thing. When you read an article or a book, such as this one, you're using the power of your focused attention to grow something.

By reading these words now, you're developing something that'll soon manifest in your physical world. Ensure that whatever content and experiences you consume are in the highest alignment with your dream life.

Like anything in your world, balance is essential. There's no need to immediately cut out all sources of information in your life that come from a frequency that you don't want to live in. You can work your way up to this, but what's most vital is that you begin to become consciously aware of how you use the power of your focused attention in daily life.

You may read books such as this one and feel empowered to manifest your dream life, and then spend the rest of your day reading the news, watching soap operas, and having conversations filled with complaints. If this is the case, you must realize that your dream life can't grow if you focus the vast majority of your attention on things that aren't in alignment with your heart's desire. You're in control of what you manifest in your life.

Knowing how much power you hold with your

focused attention is necessary to motivate yourself to choose to focus on the things you want to attract more of. There's no need to do this from a place of discipline. Instead, you'll actively choose to focus on the things that grow your dream life when you realize how powerful each small action you take is.

You'll stop reading news articles written from fear when you know deep down that you're drifting farther away from manifesting your dream life every time you do so. Before you know it, you'll automatically choose to focus your attention on the things that vibrate at the same frequency as your dream life.

Every time you decide to do something that aligns with the frequency of your heart's desire, you'll feel excellent. When you bring awareness to how lower vibrational activities affect what you manifest, participating in them will no longer feel right.

You can trust your intuitive feelings and everything that your body is communicating with you. Your body has all the answers that you need in any given moment. You can think of your body as the Universe's way of communicating with you, using a tool that you can feel and act on immediately.

It's often hard to find clarity in your mind about a given situation and whether it serves your highest good, but your body will always be straightforward. Pay close attention to how your body feels as you partake in daily activities that require your focused attention. Notice how your body feels next time you're tempted to turn on the news or read a news article.

Your body is always giving you feedback and direction you can rely on. It's through your body that the Universe is most able to communicate with you. If your body suddenly starts to feel uncomfortable for seemingly no reason, there's an important message for you to receive.

Your body will never make things too uncomfortable because the Universe wants you to enjoy your life. Still, your body's painful feelings are often the only way to get your attention, which is why it's essential to stay highly attuned to your body and its messages for you. Each of these messages carries a significant gift that'll bring you closer to living in the frequency of your heart's desire.

Your body is always working for you and never against you. The more sensitive you are to your body, the less you'll need to feel intense discomfort to receive important messages from the Universe.

If you're ever feeling lots of confusion and anxiousness in your mind and body, the best thing you can do is go into nature. As soon as you become attuned to nature's frequency, you'll find immediate peace and clarity.

Nature is a safe space you can always return to. There may be some moments in your life where fear and anxiousness seem to have such a tight grip on you that it scares every bit of your being. If you experience this, it's not the Universe torturing you. Instead, it's because there's an important message for you that you can't receive in any other way.

If you feel these strong emotions, it's a great invitation to retreat into nature. If you spend time alone in nature, you'll notice any fear and anxiousness you have falls away.

You must go into nature alone because that's how you'll open yourself to receive the message that the Universe is trying to deliver to you. It can be healing to be in nature with someone you have a healthy relationship with, but to receive that important message, you must spend a large amount of your time in your energy with nobody else near you.

Like you have a uniquely intimate relationship with the Universe, you also have a special relationship with Mother Earth. By going into nature alone, you begin to cultivate this beautiful relationship.

Mother Earth loves you unconditionally. Mother Earth can heal you and make you feel at home wherever you are in this world. Growing and appreciating this relationship you have with Mother Earth is vital for you to feel grounded and safe in your life.

Suppose you didn't receive the nurturing and unconditional love you wanted as a child. In that case, you'll be grateful to discover that all of the nurturing and unconditional love you could ever need or want is available to you from Mother Earth.

To help you feel boundless love, look at Mother Earth as your Soul's mother and Father Spirit as your Soul's father. There's a great peace that comes from seeing yourself as a divine child of Mother Earth and Father Spirit.

As long as you're alive on earth, you're equally Soul and human. To find peace and joy, you must honor and respect both of these parts of yourself. If you focus too much on cultivating your connection to your Soul, you'll feel unsafe and not at home in this world. You'll also find it hard to manifest material things, people, and circumstances in your life.

If you focus too much on the human part of yourself, you'll fear death and feel that your time here on earth is pleasurable but not meaningful. You'll also have trouble connecting with the unity of all that exists and seeing love in everything that appears in your life.

On the other hand, if you cultivate and appreciate both of these essential parts of yourself, then you'll find great beauty in everything while also feeling safe and at home here on earth. You'll not fear death or life. You'll feel at a deep level that death and life need each other to exist, and you'll find your place in this beautiful cosmic and earthly dance.

Most of the people attracted to this book are more likely to lean towards the spiritual side. If this is the case for you, the most helpful thing you can do to integrate everything you've learned is to nurture your relationship with nature and your human body. Allowing yourself to experience the orgasmic pleasure of being alive will give your Soul great peace here on earth.

There's no need to judge other humans for doing and enjoying human things such as sex, eating meat, drinking alcohol, and making mistakes. If you judge others for doing these things, you also judge the human part of yourself and stop yourself from giving your humanness what it needs to thrive.

For the entire time that you're here on earth, commit to having the earthly experience. There's nothing more noble about doing without human pleasures and restricting those things to grow your spiritual practice.

If this is your path, go for it, but don't judge a fellow human who chooses to drink lots of alcohol and have casual sex. Both of these paths are equally noble. It's your life that you get to create while having this beautiful, temporary earthly experience.

Your Soul will live on for infinity. Knowing this, you're free to play and create whatever type of life you want while here on earth. By giving yourself this freedom, you'll notice that you naturally honor others walking their unique path doing whatever they want to do with their lives.

People that feel true freedom inside of themselves will always give that same freedom to others. Remember that everything in this world is an inside-out approach. If you find yourself judging others' lifestyles, that's a sign you're judging that same part of yourself that wants to be expressed.

Now that you're fully aware of the power you hold with your focused attention and the knowledge that you're both Soul and human, you're free to manifest your dream life. Consciously using this superpower of yours will inspire the Collective to wake up to their power to manifest their dream life.

You have been given a gift by being born here on earth. Receive this gift fully by showing gratitude for being alive and have fun manifesting your dream life!

ABOUT THE AUTHOR

Eric's journey started with a love for business as a kid that led him to live around the world, connecting with other like-minded people. After living in 8 countries, he had a sudden spiritual awakening during the middle of the night where he began channeling words such as, "wake up, it's all energy."

This spiritual awakening led Eric down a path of synchronicities where he completely gave up the business path and went all-in on his spiritual practices. After attending a never-ending list of spiritual classes from clairvoyant training, to breathwork, and crystal reiki meditation, Eric found his calling in the dance of life as an Author.

Now Eric spends his time writing books that empower you to reach your Soul's Highest Potential and has gained a large following on the social media app TikTok where he's sharing excerpts from his books.

STAY CONNECTED WITH THE AUTHOR

Visit the link below and enter your email to receive free previews of Eric's newest books before they're released:

www.ericjohncampbell.com

Follow Eric's TikTok account:

www.tiktok.com/@ericjohncampbell

Lightning Source UK Ltd.
Milton Keynes UK
UKHW010618090123
415042UK00002B/666

9 781087 991023